Performance Management Practitioner Series

Alternative Pay Progression Strategies: Broadbanding Applications

United States Office of Personnel Management — Human Resources Systems Service — Office of Employee Relations and Workforce Performance — Performance Management and Incentive Awards Division — Theodore Roosevelt Bldg. 1900 E Street, N.W. Washington, DC 20415-0001 — PMD-05 — April 1996

Table of Contents

Introduction

As an organization delayers its structure, establishes work teams, and embraces quality initiatives, it also may consider realigning its pay and classification system to support and promote these changes. Broadbanding is one vehicle for moving these changes forward.

This report begins by reviewing some basic aspects of compensation and broadbanding that will help clarify further discussion on pay progression strategies. (The term "pay progression" refers to how the pay rates of individual employees will be adjusted over time.) Then the report presents **three categories of pay progression strategies:**

(1) time-based, (2) performance-based, and (3) development-based. These strategies can be used singly or in combination. How an organization applies them depends on its culture, environment, work structure, and its overall goals and strategic plans. The description of each category includes: (a) organizational characteristics best suited for implementation; (b) methods for determining the amount of a pay adjustment; (c) advantages and disadvantages; and (d) examples of the pay progression strategy in practice. The effects of combining the strategies are also discussed.

Overview

The specific design features of any pay system represent pay policy choices. Those policies are realized through the specific pay administration actions taken under the system, e.g., the adjustments made to individual employees' rates of pay. Those actions, while often appearing rule-driven and rigidly constructed, nevertheless carry meaning and messages over which the pay system designers can exercise choice. This report is intended to help system designers consider what meaning and messages they may want to choose or avoid in their broadbanding systems.

As pay system designers determine their pay band structure, they may choose from a variety of strategies for determining pay progression within the bands. This aspect of pay system design in broadbanding applications is a key pay administration feature that deserves

careful consideration. Pay adjustments are typically the most frequent and most specific phenomena that employees actually experience under any compensation system, but especially a broadbanding scheme. Therefore, it is important to design and communicate their basis clearly. In addition, and perhaps more important, the pay progression scheme a system includes can most directly affect overall compensation costs.

Any discussion of pay progression in broadbanding must be anchored by some fundamental compensation concepts. It may be helpful to review some basic terminology and principles, as well as the general concepts involved in broadbanding, before describing alternative within-range pay progression strategies.

Compensation Concept

Pay Structures. Most organizations use compensation approaches under which pay rates are established in some systematic fashion. While some use systems where all employees in a job type or rank are paid at the same rate, it is far more common to see **pay ranges**, each with a minimum and maximum rate of pay, devised to cover multiple positions and employees. A set of such pay ranges is commonly called a **pay structure** or pay schedule.

One pay policy choice organizations face is where their pay will fall, on average, relative to the **market rate**. Both public and private organizations conduct wage surveys to determine the market rate for benchmark jobs. Depending on the labor supply, the qualifications required to do the work, the strategy of the organization, and other factors, organizations may choose to pay, in the aggregate, either at, below, or above the market rate. That choice carries a message about an organization's view of its place in the labor market. In private organizations, the midpoint of a pay range is usually the market rate for the job and is a critical factor in an organization maintaining a competitive pay position within the labor market (ACA/ASPA, 1988). In devising a pay structure, system designers must also make policy choices about how narrow or broad to make the pay ranges; that is, whether the maximum rate exceeds the minimum rate by a relatively small or large amount. Lately, the trend has been to broaden pay ranges.

Another key consideration for pay system design focuses on how an employee's **position-in-range** will be affected by pay progression policies. Position-in-range refers to the position of the employee's pay rate relative to the minimum rate for the range. Typically, most pay systems set pay for novice employees at a lower position-in-range and reserve rates at a higher position-in-range for skilled, experienced employees.

Base Pay Increases. There are three types of base pay increases: promotions, general increases, and within-range increases.

The first type of increase to base pay is a **promotion**. This pay increase is generally applied as an individual action and represents upward movement between pay ranges. With a promotion, the employee's actual rate of pay is increased. Policies may be set concerning minimum or maximum increases for promotions. And as with other compensation practices, an organization's policies affecting promotions carry messages. Consider the difference in "mean-ing" between a virtually automatic, but small, shift between narrow pay ranges and a highly competitive, and substantial, shift between broad, widely-spaced pay ranges.

The second type of base pay increase is a **general increase**. When a general, or across-the-board, increase is given, all employees receive the same percentage pay increase. For example, an annual adjustment (or what is commonly referred to as a cost-of-living adjustment) is a general increase.

Most private organizations do not actually grant general increases for their white collar employees. This is principally because most organizations consider performance to be a fundamental value that should drive their compensation systems to support individual pay equity. Granting general increases is not compatible conceptually with that value.

These organizations usually achieve the effect of a general increase by including it as a component of a "merit-based" within-range increase (see below). The most common practice is to apply the percentage of a general increase to the pay structure only, as a **structural increase**. That is, the minimum and maximum rates of the pay ranges will be increased, without actually adjusting the rates of pay of individual employees. (However, some organizations will automatically adjust the rate of employees paid at the minimum rate to bring them up to the newly increased minimum rate.) For the majority of employees within the pay range, individual pay adjustments that maintain their position-in-range are delivered via other within-range adjustments.

The final type of base pay increase, and the focus of this report, is the **within-range increase**. Within-range increases can be based on time, performance, the develop-ment of the employee, or a combination of any of these. Through within-range increases, employees improve their position-in-range, within the pay ranges or bands. Most private sector organizations still deliver within-range increases for white collar employees as merit increases, which typically vary by individual employees depending on performance and position-in-range. All employees who per-form even merely adequately usually end up with an adjustment at least the size of any structural increase, so that they maintain their position-in-range. However, some organiza-tions will permit employees paid near the top of the range to decelerate back toward the market rate (by delivering an adjustment smaller than the structural increase percentage) unless their performance is rated

well above average.

The pace at which within-range progression occurs, the basis for that progress, any limits on that progress, and which factors will make a difference across individual employees are the policy choices that organizations face. For example:

- What will it mean to move faster through the range, i.e., accelerate or gain posi-tion-in-range relative to other employees? *(You're an exceptional performer? You have acquired a critical job competency ahead of schedule?)*

- What will it mean to be paid above the market rate? *(You have specialized skills? You have received another longevity increase?)*

- What will it mean to be paid at the top of the range? *(You're a top performer? You've "been around the longest"?)*

- Will it be possible to decelerate within-range progress or lose position-in-range relative to other employees, and what will that mean? *(You have failed to improve performance? You haven't maintained a previous level of performance?)*

There are no predetermined answers. The pay progression alternatives discussed in this report present different possible answers. And even within a general alternative strat-egy, specific progression schemes can pro-duce different patterns of answers. Pay sys-tem designers need to consider what they want the answers to be and then choose care-fully among pay progression alternatives to achieve those answers.

AN ILLUSTRATION: THE GENERAL SCHEDULE

Pay Structure. The General Schedule (GS) is an example of a pay structure. Each of its 15 grades has a 30 percent range, that is, the maximum rate for each range is 130 percent of the value of the minimum rate. These days, 30 percent is considered a fairly narrow rate range. Under the national pay administration policy enacted through the Federal Employees Pay Comparability Act of 1990 (FEPCA), GS pay ranges are set and structured so that, under its full implementation and through the operation of locality pay adjustments for specific pay areas, the overall difference between non-Federal and Federal salaries in each pay area is no more than 5 percent of the Federal rate.

Pay Progression. A Federal employee under the General Schedule always maintains position-in-range because the annual adjustment, a structural increase, to the General Schedule is actually paid out to virtually all employees as a general increase, irrespective of other factors like performance. Although commonly referred to as a "cost-of-living increase," the General Schedule's annual adjustment is actually based on a Bureau of Labor Statistics cost-of-labor measure, the Employment Cost Index, and can also be influenced by the Federal budget.

Each General Schedule grade's range is subdivided into ten steps or fixed rates of pay. Within-range pay progression is achieved through the use of periodic step increases, or within-grade increases. Step increases generally are granted as a fixed amount throughout the range (as opposed to a fixed percentage increase) on a time schedule set by statute. The amount of a step increase, usually, is equal to one-ninth of the difference between the minimum and maximum rates for the range. This pay progression scheme includes a performance contingency component because statute also stipulates that, to be eligible for an increase, an employee must be performing at an "acceptable level of competence" (aka "ALOC").

This stable, predictable progression scheme of the General Schedule actually carries with it a meaning and message that, although now perhaps somewhat faded, underlay its original design. Progressing through fixed steps at fixed intervals that get longer over time is based on a "learning curve theory." That is, initial annual pay increases reward a substantial increase in skills, knowledge, and improved performance presumed to occur during the first few years in the grade (steps 1-4). Pay progression decelerates once full mastery is achieved (steps 4-7 delivered biannually). Finally, skill acquisition is presumed to taper off and the final step increases are granted at extended 3-year intervals to reward the loyalty, longevity, and continued mastery of long-term employees, short of promoting them. Pay progression can be accelerated for GS employees through the use of quality step increases (QSI's), i.e., additional step increases granted to exceptional performers. Taken together across all nine increments of a GS pay range, all three pay progression strategies described in this report operate to some extent: time (periodic increases), performance (ALOC requirement and QSI's), and development (skill acquisition assumed to be greatest at steps 1-4 and tapering off after step 4).

Broadbanding

Definition. Broadbanding is a pay and classification approach that combines two or more grades into broad pay bands. The term "banding" is also applied to the notion of grouping jobs horizontally. That is, specific position classification series may be consolidated into broader job "families." That form of banding, however, is not the subject of this report, and the term will be used here to mean vertical, or pay grade, banding.

A 1992 private sector survey conducted by Hewitt Associates reports that there are almost as many variations of broadbanding as there are organizations using it. The survey also showed that fully half of all companies that use broadbanding cover less than 10 percent of their employee population in the banding system (Braddick et al., 1992; Gerson, 1992). The variety of broadbanding approaches in use indicates that there is *not* one universal model. In fact, many consultants stress the importance of tailoring the broadbanding system to the needs of the organization (Gerson, 1992; Hay Group, 1992; LeBlanc, 1992).

Base Pay Increases. Of the three types of pay increases discussed earlier, promotion increases do not occur as frequently in a broadbanding system as they do in narrow-range grade systems because there are fewer levels to which employees can be promoted. Organizations can determine a minimum and/or maximum percentage increase for promotions. For example, the Department of Defense Nonappropriated Fund (DOD NAF) broadbanding system requires at least a 6 percent pay increase for a promotion from one band to the next higher band. (Assignment to another position within the same band is not considered a promotion.) No maximum promotion increase is set because tight budget constrictions control costs.

With respect to general increases, an organization moving to a broadbanding scheme will need to address the policy question of whether to deliver any structural increase to the employees in the bands. That is, should an automatic, general, across-the-board pay increase be granted to all employees, or should the aggregate funding for such a general increase be included as part of a total salary increase budget that is actually distributed to employees as part of their individual within-range increases?

Finally, broadbanding systems offer an opportunity to revisit the meaning and messages of within-range adjustments. Of particular importance from a cost-control standpoint is a system's policy about access to the maximum rate in the band. The Hewitt survey and other consultants found that a few organizations were moving into a "second generation" approach for broad-banding where target zones within each band are developed for specific jobs, skills, or competencies in order to avoid moving too far from market-based pricing. Some organizations used the midpoints of the bands as journeyman target levels, with only exceptional performers allowed to move past the mid-point. Most organizations, however, do not put official limits within the bands on income potential (Gerson, 1992; Hay Group, 1992).

Organizational Characteristics. Although it recommended broadbanding as one alternative to the current Federal classification system, Vice President Gore's Report of the National Performance Review implies that broadbanding may not work for everyone (NPR, 1993). Private consultants and other Federal managers who have voiced their opinions share this view (Gerson, 1992; Hay Group, 1992; LeBlanc, 1992). Organi-zations that are likely to be most successful at implementing a well-designed broadband-ing program have many of the character-istics listed below:

- The organization is reengineering work, flattening its structure, introducing cross training, eliminating functional boundaries, and increasing employees' decision-making responsibilities (Hofrichter, 1993).

- The organization has a strong performance-based culture (Hay Group, 1992), and an effective performance management system is in place (Braddick et al., 1992; Hay Group, 1992).

- The organization is looking to support a new culture and most likely has just exper-ienced a precipitous event (Braddick et al., 1992).

- Top management strongly supports the broadbanding system (Braddick et al., 1992; Hay Group, 1992).

- Effective communication channels exist within the organization (Braddick et al., 1992), and high levels of trust and under-standing exist among employees and man-agement (Hay Group, 1992).

- Line managers are skilled at setting and managing employee pay (Braddick et al., 1992).

- The organization has a good market data system in order to determine market rates for setting pay and for adjusting pay scales (Gerson, 1992; Hay Group, 1992).

- An organization with a well-designed, extremely accurate budgeting and allocation system is more likely to implement a broadbanding system successfully because budget is a significant factor in determining base pay increases (Hay Group, 1992). A large number of organizations allocate a specific percentage of total payroll for base pay increases in order to ensure that budgets are met and maintained. (The Navy demonstration project and DOD NAF employees under performance-based pay progression are examples of salary budgeting.)

- Many managers and consultants believe that organizations should have a variable pay program also, since base pay is only one part of a compensation strategy. Variable pay, group incentives, gainsharing, etc. can all affect levels of employee performance and should not be left out of the picture (McNally, 1992).

Survey of Current Broadbanding Prac-tice. In 1993, the American Compensation Association sponsored a research project conducted by Hewitt Associates to survey broadbanding practice. The study report, *Broadbanding Design, Alternatives, and Practices* (Abosch & Hand, 1994), provides a comprehensive look at experience to date and identifies emerging trends and issues.

Summary. An organization will need to consider many factors carefully before adopt-ing broadbanding. Broadbanding will not meet the needs of every organization. When the compensation strategy is linked with most other organizational strategies, the systems will work toward a common goal, not work against each other.

Alternative Strategies for Pay Progression

Time-Based Pay Progression

Description. In a time-based pay system, base pay increases rely solely on time spent at a pay level.

Organizational Characteristics. Time-based pay progression works best in organizations that have repetitive, routine jobs where there is small potential for varying performance (Greene, 1991). Also, because union leaders often favor a time-based system, this type of strategy may work best in organizations with a strong union influence. This strategy may not be the best choice for organizations that want to emphasize the importance of performance or employee development.

Methods. Organizations that use time-based pay progression usually advance employees a predetermined or negotiated percentage annually, similar to a step system. A variation of the fixed percentage method schedules higher percentage pay increases during the first few advancement periods, or more frequent adjustments, to recognize the initial sharp rise of the learning curve.

Advantages.

- A time-based pay progression strategy allows an organization to predict costs with more certainty (Greene, 1991).
- Costs can be controlled more easily by adjusting the percentage increase given.
- The measurement device that triggers the pay adjustments is well-accepted and completely noncontroversial. (Marking days off a calendar stimulates none of the tur-

moil that performance appraisal ratings can stir up!)

Disadvantages. There are a number of disadvantages to using a time-based pay progression strategy, especially for organizations encouraging quality and continuous improvement.

- A time-based pay strategy sends the mes-sage that performance does not matter.
- Reducing the salience of performance promotes mediocre performance and top performers usually leave for other organizations that will recognize their contributions.
- De-emphasizing performance also encourages employees to protect their turf, further hindering cooperation and organizational improvement.
- Finally, employees who have worked a number of years at the same job may have reached the top of their pay level (Greene, 1991).

***Example.* Pacer Share.** The Pacer Share demonstration project at McClellan Air Force Base in Sacramento, California, used automatic annual pay increases. Basing its strategies on Dr. W. Edwards Deming's management philosophies, the project eliminated individual performance appraisal and based all pay increases on seniority. Employees received between 1 and 3 percent pay increases annually without variation, depending on which tercile of the band they fell within. On top of that, they also received the same amount of annual adjustment that was given other Federal employees. (The band structure was also adjusted upward.) This double increase is very similar to the current Federal pay system with its steps and annual adjustments. Pacer Share relied on gainsharing to promote improved performance.

An employee survey revealed that there was low satisfaction with the Pacer Share pay advancement strategy. The survey also showed that Pacer Share supervisors felt little authority to affect the pay of subordinates (Schay, 1993). Because of these results, evaluators recommended that Pacer Share management consider modifying their pay progression process by including a pay-for-performance component using process improvement as a measure (OPM, 1992). No changes were made, however, because management felt that adding a performance element to the process would have contradicted the basic elements of the Deming philosophy upon which the project was based. The Pacer Share demonstration project expired at the end of its 5-year statutory test period in February 1993.

Performance-Based Pay Progression

A Note about Performance Management. The term "performance management" often connotes performance appraisal **only**, when in fact it usually encompasses much more. Title 5 of the Code of Federal Regulations defines performance management as "the systematic process by which an agency integrates performance, pay, and awards systems with its basic management functions for the purpose of improving individual and organization effectiveness in the accomplishment of agency mission and goals" (5 CFR 430.102). Performance management includes processes for performance planning, assessment, incentives, and recognition.

The literature on broadbanding often refers to a "successful," "effective," or "strong" performance management system as critical for a positive broadbanding experience. A successful performance management system will have an effective assessment process that establishes work objectives and makes credible distinctions among multiple levels of performance. Assessment should accurately measure current performance levels and contain mechanisms for reinforcing strengths, identifying deficiencies and providing feedback to employees so that they may improve future performance (Schneier et al., 1982). A successful performance management system will also have an effective reward system that recognizes outstanding performance through monetary and nonmonetary rewards. These rewards provide incentives to employees to improve and maintain high levels of performance. In a successful performance management system, it should be clear to all participants that good and outstanding performers are recognized and rewarded more than average performers. It should also be evident that the system positively affects organizational performance.

Description. Performance-based pay progression strategies include a wide variety of approaches that all use the employee's level of performance to determine the amount of pay increase. Performance-based progression systems usually allow a wide spread in the percentage pay increase possible, with 0 percent given to marginal performers and up to 20-25 percent for top performers.

Organizational Characteristics. Performance-based pay progression works best in organizations that already have a culture that encourages improved performance. Despite Dr. Deming's viewpoints on performance appraisal (Deming, 1982; Scholtes, 1987), performance assessment can be a beneficial process and can mesh well with quality and continuous improvement (Graber et al., 1992).

Performance-based pay strategies work best in organizations that have strong and successful performance management systems. Employee involvement in the development of the appraisal system, from inception to implementation, should be high. This will promote credibility and encourage employee acceptance. Also, managers and supervisors should have adequate training in performance assessment (Braddick et al., 1992; Greene, 1991; NRC, 1991). Performance-based pay strategies are only as successful as the performance appraisal systems on which they depend.

Performance-based systems need adequate funding. Salary increases and/or bonuses should be meaningful to employees and commensurate with their contributions (PFPLMC, 1991). In the private sector, performance-based pay systems are most successful where managers have the flexibility or discretion to differentiate between the pay increase given to top performers and that given to good performers, and the option to dismiss poor performers (NRC, 1991).

The U.S. Office of Personnel Management (OPM) conducted a survey of Federal employees in 1992 that included questions about performance management. The survey found that nearly 97 percent of Federal employees believe that the quality of their work should be important in determining their rating, with 82 percent preferring an increase in base pay as their performance reward. This suggests potential employee acceptance of future performance-based systems since employees approve of using performance as a factor for determining pay. However, only 48 percent perceive that they will receive a pay raise or cash award if they perform exceptionally well (OPM, 1992). This

illuminates a weakness in the current Federal performance management system and suggests that future performance-based systems should focus on employee buy-in, trust in the system, and good communication.

Method. A wide range of performance-based methods can be used by organizations for determining individual pay increases, from issuing only broad guidelines with no salary increase limits to issuing specific amounts of pay increases for specific rating levels. For example, some organizations have allowed the first-line supervisors to determine the amount of pay increases based on the employee's performance, as long as the supervisor stays within budgetary limitations. Other organizations have developed a complex rating and ranking system with a matrix of fixed percentages established for each performance rating level. Often a time factor is built into performance-based systems where pay increases can only occur annually. However, some organizations place no time limitations at all; theoretically, an employee could receive a pay raise every day of the year. (The organizations without time limitations generally have strict budgetary limitations, thereby precluding the abuse of pay raises.)

These methods can be used in conjunction with target zones and midpoint strategies. They can also grant general, across-the-board increases that are given to all employees who at least perform at a certain level. However, general increases given to everyone regardless of performance are not conceptually compatible with performance-based systems (ACA/ASPA, 1988) and are not commonly found in the private sector.

Advantages.

- Pay-for-performance systems reinforce the message to employees that good performance is important to the organization.

- Employees say they want performance to influence pay.
- Merit pay can have positive effects on individual job performance (NRC, 1991).
- If pay differentiation between top performers and mid- to low-performers is significant, the prospect of receiving a meaningful reward can serve as an incentive to perform at top levels.

Disadvantages.
- The evidence shows that performance-based within-range progression systems are costly. At the same time, there is no evidence that they are effective tools for increasing organizational performance (NRC, 1991).
- If there is little difference between the increases top performers and poor performers receive, employees have little incentive to perform well (Brookes, 1993).
- If the organization does not have a credible performance appraisal system, the basis for determining pay progression is weak.
- In addition, if the appraisal system as applied fails to make distinctions among performers (e.g., 99+ percent rated "pass"), the progression scheme reverts in effect to a time-based strategy.

Examples. **Navy Demonstration (China Lake).** The Navy project uses a broadbanding system that directly links pay increases to performance rating. China Lake uses a five-level rating system that ties employee job duties to organizational goals. With a salary increase budget of 2.4 percent of payroll, managers determine base pay increases or can give cash awards in lieu of a salary increase. Managers can give from 0 percent to 6 percent in pay increases plus comparability, which has averaged 3.5 percent between 1980 and 1990 (Schay, 1993). Pay points or increments are determined for each band. These points/increments are equal to a certain percentage of the band. Comparability pay (the General Schedule annual pay adjustment and, at one project site, the locality pay adjustment) is also dependent on performance. Using a five-level rating scale, the payout matrix rewards the highest rated employees with a comparability adjustment plus either four or three points/increments, while employees rated "3" receive comparability plus one or zero increments. The position of these employees in the range advances. Meanwhile, the lowest-rated employees may receive nothing and thereby lose position-in-range (OPM, 1984).

The Navy's banding system has been very successful in balancing higher starting salaries with slower pay progression. During the first 5 years, pay progression under bands has been slower than under the General Schedule system where employees tend to start with lower salaries but move up quickly due to annual promotions which can involve 20 percent pay increases. At the Navy project, trading off higher starting salaries against slower initial pay progression is an effective strategy that has resulted in improved recruitment and retention of quality employees (Schay et al., 1992).

The National Institute of Standards and Technology Demonstration (NIST).
The NIST project also uses a broadbanding system. Originally, the project's performance management system used five rating levels, comparable to the Performance Management and Recognition System (PMRS) for Federal managers in grades 13, 14, and 15. However, in 1991, NIST adapted its system to include some of the characteristics of a two-level rating system. Appraisal elements are awarded points with 100 total points possible. An employee who scores below 40 points is unsatisfactory and will receive no base pay increase. The amount of pay increase the employee receives depends on the employee's

rating, his/her ranking compared to other employees, and into which tercile of the band the employee falls (Reynolds et al., 1992; Schay, 1993).

NIST uses a pay matrix that places limits on the amount of base pay increase employees may receive (see below). The specific amount chosen from the range shown on the pay matrix depends on the ranking of the employee based on the number of points (40-100) from the appraisal rating. To recognize the initial learning curve and move employees quickly to the market rate, the limits in the first tercile are much higher than the limits in the second and third terciles. Since 1988 when the project began, NIST salaries have increased about 4 percent more under broad

NIST Pay Increase Matrix

Pay-for-Performance Payout Matrix				
Career Path	Pay Band	Pay Range Intervals and Ranges of Salary Increase Percentages		
		Tercile 1	Tercile 2	Tercile 3
ZA Administrative Pay Plan	I II III IV V	0-14% 0-20% 0-15% 0-10% 0- 6%	0-12% 0-16% 0-12% 0- 8% 0- 5%	0-7% 0-8% 0-7% 0-6% 0-4%
ZP Scientific and Engineering Pay Plan	I II III IV V	0-14% 0-20% 0-15% 0-10% 0- 6%	0-12% 0-16% 0-12% 0- 8% 0- 5%	0-7% 0-8% 0-7% 0-6% 0-4%
ZS Support Pay Plan	I II III IV V	0-12% 0-12% 0- 8% 0- 7% 0- 6%	0-10% 0- 8% 0- 6% 0- 5% 0- 4%	0-7% 0-6% 0-5% 0-3% 0-3%
ZT Scientific and Engineering Technician Pay Plan	I II III IV V	0-12% 0-12% 0- 8% 0- 7% 0- 6%	0-10% 0- 8% 0- 6% 0- 5% 0- 4%	0-7% 0-6% 0-5% 0-3% 0-3%

(Reynolds et al., 1992)

banding than the salaries of a comparison group under the General Schedule system (Schay, 1993).

Employee and supervisor surveys show that employees feel that higher performance is better rewarded, that more employees are satisfied with their pay, and that supervisors feel they have more control over their employees' pay and are better able to reward them (Reynolds et al., 1992).

Department of Defense (DOD) Nonappropriated Fund (NAF) Employees.
DOD NAF employees (except for craft and trades) are under a six-band broadbanding system very similar to the Navy project. Commands can determine their own policy for granting discretionary pay increases. DOD has regulated

that the general increase (annual pay adjustment) will increase the minimum and maximum rates of the bands as well as employees' individual pay rates so that employees do not lose position-in-range.

Pay progression within the bands must be negotiated with local unions at each command or installation since NAF employees are not covered by title 5 pay regulations and must bargain pay and benefits. Discretionary pay increases can be based on increased job responsibility, on the performance rating, or can be given for other reasons. Pay increases must be recommended by the supervisor and approved by a higher-level manager. Budget limitations similar to those in the Navy project are in place and are a key factor in determining pay increases. Despite the various reasons pay increases can be granted, DOD defines the NAF system as performance-based.

U.S. General Accounting Office (GAO).

About 74 percent of GAO's employees (evaluators and attorneys) are in a broad-banding system. General increases (annual pay or comparability adjustments) are given to everyone and are not tied to performance. The minimums and maximums of the bands are also adjusted so that employees maintain their position-in-range.

A management review group (MRG) panel determines individual pay increases by considering four information sources: (1) the performance appraisal, which has ratings for seven critical factors but no overall rating; (2) a contribution statement, which is the staff member's view of his/her contributions; (3) panelists' knowledge of the individual's and the group's work; and (4) the discussions during the MRG meetings covering the performance and contributions of each staff member. Based on data gathered from the information sources, the MRG places broadbanded employees into four pay categories: Exceptional, Meritorious, Commendable, or Acceptable. A merit increase matrix specifies percentage increases allowable to each pay category as well as bonuses (see next page). There is a direct correlation between pay category and amount of merit increase, with Exceptional employees receiving around 4 to 5 percentage points higher pay increases than Acceptable employees.

GAO management feels the system is successful. Employee surveys show dissatisfaction with requirements that at least 10 percent of employees fall into the Acceptable pay category and that only two-thirds of the employees may receive bonuses. Because of recom-mendations made recently by a TQM team, these limitations have been eliminated.

GAO 1992 Merit Increase and Bonus Tables

Band	Placement of Salary in Range	Performance Group		
		Exceptional	Meritorious/ Commendable	Acceptable
I	1st Half of Range	6.0%	3.5%	1.0%
	2nd Half of Range	4.0%	2.0%	0.0%
	Bonus Range (Exceptional/Meritorious Only)	5-7%	2-4%	N/A
II	1st Quarter of Range	6.0%	3.5%	1.0%
	2nd Quarter of Range	5.0%	2.5%	0.5%
	3rd Quarter of Range	4.5%	2.0%	0.0%
	4th Quarter of Range	4.0%	1.5%	0.0%
	Bonus Range (Exceptional/Meritorious Only)	5-7%	2-4%	N/A
III	1st Third of Range	6.0%	3.5%	1.0%
	2nd Third of Range	4.75%	2.5%	0.5%
	3rd Third of Range	4.0%	1.5%	0.0%
	Bonus Range (Exceptional/Meritorious Only)	5-7%	2-4%	N/A

(GAO, 1992)

A GAO representative reports that since the system has only been in place 4 years, the agency has not yet had the problem of people "maxing out" in their bands, but it might be a problem in the future. If this occurs, a GAO manager states that GAO will likely give bonuses to those who have reached the top of their pay bands in place of base pay increases.

Data General. The Data General Corporation implemented a broadbanding system for 3,000 of its exempt employees. Five "career bands" cover first-line supervisors up to and including the Chief Executive Officer. Bands 1 through 4 are merit eligible, which means that employees in these bands are eligible for base salary increases or cash awards based on several factors. These factors are: (a) the market value of the job performed; (b) the salary of peers; (c) a written performance appraisal; and (d) budgetary limitations. The system is extremely flexible in that no minimum or maximum pay limits are assigned to the career bands and that current,

undocumented performance is taken into account along with the formal performance ratings. No general pay adjustments are given to all employees. There are no established percentages of increase given for particular ratings. (Band 5 salary increases for top executives depend on other factors.)

A Data General representative stated that it took 2 years to design and implement this program. The most difficult issues were pay comparability (internal and external) and employee buy-in.

General Electric (GE). Many of GE's divisions use broadbanding systems. One particular division has collapsed 14 non-executive grades into 4 broad bands that cover 97 percent of its employees. When GE hires a new employee, they place the employee within the band based on the skills and knowledge of the employee. Job descriptions have been eliminated and replaced by job objectives which are determined by customer satisfaction surveys. There have been no annual adjustments made to the bands or to employees' base pay. Annually, managers appraise employees, give each a performance grade (A, B, C, or D), and then determine pay increases based on that grade, budget limitations, and the market data for benchmark jobs. A GE representative says the program has been very successful because it streamlines management processes (through the elimination of job descriptions) and provides greater flexibility for getting the work done. One of the greatest challenges to both managers and employees is to erase the stigma associated with not receiving a promotion.

Pratt & Whitney. Pratt & Whitney reduced the number of salary levels from 11 to 6 and cut the number of job descriptions by more than half. This was done to support and promote a flatter organization structure that placed a greater emphasis on cross-functional and matrix-type team approaches to problem solving. Performance ratings, budget limitations and market value determine the amount of a pay increase. No general annual adjustment to base pay is made. Human resources staff are under increased pressure to maintain external market relationships. The company expects that the reduced number of grades eventually will lead to a need for fewer management layers and will improve vertical communications overall (Eyes, 1993).

A Pratt & Whitney representative reports that the company is still downsizing and changing its structure. Soon Pratt & Whitney will decentralize almost all personnel management functions, allowing each division to determine its internal management systems.

Performance Management and Recognition System (PMRS). PMRS was a merit pay system for mid-level managers in the Federal Government that covered supervisors and management officials in General Schedule positions at grades 13 through 15 (OPM, 1995). It was

established in 1986 as a successor to an earlier merit pay system for those same employees, which had been enacted as part of a major reform of the Federal civil service system in 1978. PMRS terminated as of November 1, 1993, and PMRS employees returned to the pay adjustment policies and procedures of the General Schedule.

Technically, PMRS is not an example of pay progression through wide pay ranges. However, the Federal experience with PMRS is instructive of the effects of per-formance-based within-range adjustments operating with only limited controls. The principal features of PMRS pay adjustments were set in statute, along with a requirement to use a five-level performance appraisal system and to grant rating-based lump-sum performance awards. Receipt of the general increase was contingent on performance being rated Fully Successful. When that general increase was withheld, a poor performer's pay rate could slip below the minimum rate for the grade, and that did occur in a handful of cases.

Annual within-range adjustments were driven by a merit increase matrix (see next page) that combined performance rating and position-in-range, as prescribed in law. A full merit increase was equivalent to the periodic step increase other General Schedule employees received. Because merit increases were annual, PMRS employees in the upper two-thirds of the pay range received increases in their rates of basic pay in advance of their GS counterparts, who had 2- and 3-year waiting periods. A merit increase could not result in a pay rate above the maximum rate for the grade; the merit increase would be reduced by whatever amount would leave the resulting pay rate at the maximum rate. That limitation was one of the few cost controls in the system.

The relationship among three possible sources of cost control salary increase budgets, payout formulas, and performance rating distributions is clearly illustrated by the PMRS design and

Performance Management and Recognition System
Merit Increase Matrix

PERFORMANCE RATING LEVEL	1ST TERCILE	2ND TERCILE	3RD TERCILE
OUTSTANDING	Full Merit Increase 3.33%-3.03%	Full Merit Increase 3.03%-2.78%	Full Merit Increase 2.78%-0.00%
EXCEEDS FULLY SUCCESSFUL	Full Merit Increase 3.33%-3.03%	½ Merit Increase 1.51%-1.39%	½ Merit Increase 1.39%-0.00%
FULLY SUCCESSFUL	Full Merit Increase 3.33%-3.03%	½ Merit Increase 1.51%-1.39%	Merit Increase 0.93%-0.00%
MINIMALLY SUCCESSFUL	- 0 -	- 0 -	- 0 -
UNACCEPTABLE	- 0 -	- 0 -	- 0 -

(U.S. Office of Personnel Management, 1995)

experience. In addition to prescribing the merit matrix, the law also prohibited forced distributions of performance ratings. Until 1991, a combination of two other legal provisions (mandated 2 percent-of-basic-pay cash awards for PMRS employees rated Outstanding and a limit on spending by each agency for such cash awards of 1.5 percent-of-payroll) technically meant that Outstanding ratings could not be granted to more than 75 percent of PMRS employees in an agency. In 1991, even that control was lifted when the 2 percent cash award requirement was removed. This combination of a statutory payout matrix with no performance rating controls resulted in an uncontrollable salary increase budget. Once the rating was given, the pay increase was an entitlement. The designers of PMRS likely never envisioned the rating inflation that occurred unabated during the PMRS years and that trickled down inexorably into the rank-and-file (OPM, 1995). Between 1985 and 1993, the percentage of PMRS employees who were rated Outstanding increased from 20.7 percent to 41.1 percent, while the percentage of PMRS employees rated Fully Successful decreased from 30.1 percent to

14.0 percent. The direct result of this rating inflation was ever-increasing costs in terms of the merit increases that those ratings earned. Because the payout formulas were fixed by law and the ratings distribution was not controllable (save by an act of will to raise performance standards), the salary increase budget could not be controlled.

An indirect effect of the rating inflation is perhaps even more instructive for designing within-range pay progression schemes. By 1992, after only 6 years of operation, the PMRS population began to show signs of significant "maxing out." That is, more and more employees had reached a pay rate very high in their grade range and were bumping up against the maximum rates. At the individual level, the effect is that employees started getting "shortchanged" in their merit increases because those mandated increasesmust be reduced by the amount in excess of a pay adjustment up to the maximum rate. Between 1988 and 1993, the number of PMRS employees who had reached a position high enough in the pay range where they faced being so "shortchanged" had increased by more than 50 percent, while the total PMRS population had only increased by 23 percent. Some of this "maxing out" effect under PMRS occurred due to the narrow General Schedule pay ranges and in fact is a principal source of the impetus to move to pay banding. However, PMRS illustrates how the onset of this effect was accelerated by phenomena independent of range width.

First, the unabated rating inflation was driving employees through the pay range at a much faster rate. A PMRS employee rated Outstanding every year would have moved from the minimum to the maximum rate in 9 years, compared with the 18-year time frame the General Schedule uses. Technically, a continually Outstanding GS employee could move that quickly or even quicker by getting a quality step increase every year in addition to normal periodic step increases. However, in practice this does not occur and, if it did, would be a matter of management discretion, not legal entitlement.

A second, more subtle source of the "maxing out" effect was the smaller structural adjustments that began in the early 1990's and may likely continue for some time. Anytime the average employee percentage within-range adjustment exceeds the size of the structural adjustment, the average position-in-range an indicator of the degree of the effect goes up.

This was clearest in the year when there was no general, structural increase to the General Schedule. The October 1993 pay adjustments were followed by a 0 percent general increase in January 1994. Subsequent pay increases granted within an unmoved structure raised average position-in-range.

A final source of rising average position-in-range was the general labor economy of the late 1980's and early 1990's. Turnover, hiring, and promotions had all slowed considerably. In the aggregate, this left posi-tion-in-range climbing on average, since fewer people higher in the range had been leaving and fewer people had been hired or promoted into the lower part of the range. The effect of the current mid- and late 1990's downsizing of the Federal Government remains to be seen.

The PMRS experience illustrates the effects of failing to incorporate appropriate sources of control into a within-range pay progression design. In retrospect, the absolute prohibitions of some of those potential sources of control, such as adjusting payout formulas or limiting the use of high, expensive performance ratings, appear questionable. Those prohibitions may have been well-intentioned at the outset, in the spirit of building acceptance of PMRS. However, their cumulative effect, in the absence of any self-imposed restraint by senior management on rating inflation, was negative for the system's credibility and cost-effectiveness.

Development-Based Pay Progression

Currently, several private sector pay progression strategies are similar to each other but fundamentally different from time-based and performance-based strategies. For the purposes of this report, these "different" pay strategies can be categorized as development-based pay. Whereas time-based and performance-based pay systems reward the good performance of a particular job or the time spent in the job, development-based pay progression rewards the employee's development and demonstrated proficiency in newly-learned knowledge, skills, abilities, value-adding characteristics, and/or other attributes. This fundamental change, from paying for the job to paying for skills, works successfully in high-involvement companies. These companies usually have: (a) delayered organizations; (b) self-managed work teams; (c) extensive communication of business information; (d) high levels of training; and (e) innovative reward systems.

Skill-based pay and competency-based pay are two compensation strategies that fall into the development-based category. They are very similar–so similar that Gerald E. Ledford, Jr., a leading expert on skill-based pay, stated in a telephone conversation with the authors that the two terms are used interchangeably, with skill-based pay usually applied to blue collar work and competency-based pay applied to white-collar work. However, the Hay Group draws specific distinctions between the two. Because the literature distinguishes between the two, this report describes each approach separately. Nevertheless, many of the methods, organizational characteristics, and advantages and disadvantages are the same for both approaches.

Skill-Based Pay Progression

Description. A skill-based pay system bases salary increases on how many skills employees have or how many jobs they can do (Lawler et al., 1993). This requires organizations to shift from managing jobs to managing people and skill sets. This type of pay is different from performance-based pay because this strategy pays the person for the skills and knowledge that they have, not the performance they've demonstrated, the duties they perform, or the job they encumber. Skill-based pay requires that the organ-ization identify the skills needed to perform its work (using skill units or blocks), develop ways to determine whether an individual has learned the skills, and ensure that the skills fit its strategic plan and work design. Employees are usually hired at a minimum, developmental wage, with pay increases dependent on skills learned and demonstrated. The organization must make it clear to employees how acquiring skills will affect their pay (Lawler, 1992).

A survey sponsored by the American Compensation Association (ACA) found that skill-based pay plans typically are used in a wide variety of industries and technologies and that these plans apply to a wide range of jobs (although supervisory and management jobs are usually excluded). The survey also found that these plans are very successful and promote flexibility, productivity, and employee growth (Jenkins et al., 1992).

The ACA survey also found that although most organizations that use skill-based pay do not have unions, the ones that do had a high degree of success in gaining union buy-in and support. Legal problems were also not an issue. There were very few lawsuits filed on skill-based pay issues. The cases that were filed were decided in favor of the organization (Jenkins et al., 1992).

Skill-based pay systems do not necessarily need to include or exclude the idea of paying for individual performance. They are neutral on the point of whether individuals should receive more pay depending on how well they perform a particular skill. They deal only with the issue of whether someone can perform a job. But it is quite possible to assess how well individuals perform each of the skills and combine that with a skill-based system (Lawler, 1992).

Organization Characteristics. Skill-based pay works best in organizations where jobs are highly interdependent, cooperation and support are required, flexibility of work assignment is needed, and the skills are reasonably stable (Greene, 1991; Lawler, 1992).

Organizations should also have good skills measurement systems as well as organization performance measures. Managers need to be able to financially justify higher wages through improved organizational performance, better quality products, or higher profits. It is also helpful feedback for employees to see that their added skills make a difference in the organization's performance (Verespej, 1992).

Some organizations using skill-based pay have developed problems with their systems because they had inadequate or faulty performance appraisal systems (Jenkins et al., 1992). The assessment process either was not accepted by employees, had meaningless performance distinctions, had incompetent or biased raters, or had other deficiencies. Performance assessment is important to a skill-based system because once skills are learned, employees must be assessed on their performance of the new skills to ensure competency. Good performance management systems are necessary for successful skill-based compensation.

In a survey of Fortune 1000 companies in the U.S. by Edward E. Lawler and his colleagues, the following patterns among organizations using skill-based pay were found:

- 51 percent of the responding companies used skill-based pay for at least some of their employees (an increase of more than 25 percent over 3 years). The percentage of employees covered in these companies was less than 20 percent.

- Most companies using skill-based pay also used employee involvement practices, such as participation groups, job enrichment, and self-managed work teams. Lawler and his colleagues argue that skill-based pay is an important component of employee involvement systems.

- Most organizations that use skill-based pay also use TQM as a management practice.

- Skill-based pay practices are especially likely to be adopted by companies that feel strong competitive pressures in the marketplace.

- Firms that have removed management layers during recent years are most likely to adopt skill-based pay practices.

- 59 percent of companies with skill-based pay said they used gainsharing or other incentive plans, while only 19 percent of those who do not use skill-based pay used gainsharing.

- 67 percent of current users planned to increase their use of skill-based pay, while 33 percent planned to stay the same (Lawler et al., 1993).

Method. The organization must define skill sets or skill blocks required for its work. It must also assign a monetary value to each skill set/block. In order to earn a pay increase, the employee must demonstrate competency in the new skills. Supervisors and/or peers assess competency. In some organizations, once the employee is certified, pay is increased. In other organizations, pay increases are confined to annual reviews.

Advantages.

- Skill-based pay reinforces employee involvement and a participative culture. Organizations using total quality management principles and forms of employee involvement find that employees tend to make greater contributions when there is an incentive to increase their job skills and knowledge (Greene, 1991; Lawler, 1992).
- A skill-based system gives managers flexibility in job assignment because it encourages employees to cross-train, both vertically and horizontally. This can lead to leaner staffing, especially among production employees, and increases bench strength (Greene, 1991; Lawler, 1992).
- If the organization can make use of skilled

people in ways that add significant value to the product, then total labor costs can be lower than with a traditional pay system (Lawler, 1992). So far, the experience of companies using skill-based pay plans indicates they actually cut costs, despite increased wages (Jenkins et al., 1992; Lawler et al., 1993; Verespej, 1992).

- Using skill-based pay for all employees puts everyone on the same footing and creates a homogeneous culture. It is also a good way to deal with the problems of career progres-sion that are created by a flat organization structure (Lawler, 1992).

Disadvantages.

- The system encourages employees to become more valuable to the organization as a basis for being paid more (Lawler, 1992). If not carefully controlled, costs will escalate quickly (Greene, 1991). Organizations must show productivity gains to justify the higher wages paid under a skill-based pay system (Verespej, 1992).
- It may not work for all occupations within an organization. Can the organization's culture support multiple approaches to administering pay? (Greene, 1991). Also, there has been a problem in some organizations with resentment among employees not covered under the plan (Jenkins et al., 1992).
- Employees may top out in their pay range (Lawler, 1992).
- Skill-based pay makes market comparisons of jobs difficult (Lawler, 1992).
- It requires organizations to keep track of exactly who is qualified on all of the different tasks and the different pay rates (Lawler, 1992).

Competency-Based Pay Progression

Description. The Hay Group report defines competencies as "the set of skills, knowledge, abilities, characteristics, and other attributes that, in the right combination for the right set of circumstances, will [lead to] superior performance." Competency-based pay is similar to skill-based pay in that it bases rewards on learned skills and knowledge. However, two other deeper levels of behavior are considered: (a) the type of self-image, work attitudes, and values needed to perform a job; and (b) the basic motives and traits that cause some people to be more driven and achievement-oriented than others (Hay Group, 1992; Hofrichter, 1993).

In short, just because a person has the skills to do the job doesn't ensure that he/she will be a top performer. Certain characteristics, such as initiative, teamwork effectiveness, and leadership, to name a few, are key strategies used by top performers (Froiland, 1993). Companies that use competency-based pay encourage and promote superior performance over average performance, by rewarding demonstrated competencies (Hay Group, 1992).

Organization Characteristics. An organ-ization considering adopting a competency-based system should have a job evaluation system, good market data, a highly specific performance measurement system that includes group contributions such as 360-degree or peer appraisal, and a flexible automated salary administration system. An organization should also be delayered, with relatively few hierarchies in its structure, and it should accomplish most of its work through teams. Organizations must also establish competencies that are validated as predictors

of success for each type of job or pay level (Hay Group, 1992; Hofrichter, 1993).

Method. The organization must first establish valid competencies for job levels, broad-bands, or even for the organization overall. The Hay Group states that the competency-based approach awards pay in two stages: (1) up to market level for demonstrating job understanding and satisfactory performance of skills; and (2) beyond the market level for growth in key competencies that create real value and advance the organization (Hay Group, 1992).

The Hay Group recommends that organizations that want to use a competency-based pay system should phase it in slowly. During the first phase, the organization should emphasize the market rate for satisfactory performance, with above-market-rate salaries for superior performance (i.e., begin with a successful performance-based system). A 360-degree or peer appraisal approach should be established, and variable pay should be tied to results. In the second phase, the organization can begin incorporating competencies into the assessment process. In the final phase, the organization can weigh competencies more heavily (Hay Group, 1992).

Advantages.
- Competency-based adjustments focus employee attention on improving work strategies that support the organization's core mission and capabilities.
- Superior performance through developing competencies becomes a goal that supports overall strategic plans.
- Organizations can place more emphasis on the added value workers contribute as they broaden the scope of their jobs.
- Improving employees' competencies supports involvement initiatives, delayered work structures, and teamwork.

Disadvantages.

- Researching, developing and validating competencies takes a great deal of time, money and effort. (The Employment Service at OPM has a database called MOSAIC that lists competencies for most Federal positions at all levels of development.)
- Payroll costs may increase dramatically.

Examples of Development-Based Pay Progression.

DOD Child Development Centers (CDC).
To improve the quality of the workforce in its child care centers, DOD placed its nonappropriated fund child care givers (called program assistants) into a broadband system that has a structured training program. Completion of twelve training modules determines salary increases, with the first two modules as required training and the rest as optional. As employees complete a module, CDC directors can increase base pay as a reward (although this is not required). If a program assistant completes all the modules, they receive a promotion into the next band. Many CDC directors have found that increasing pay as modules are completed encourages employees to increase their skills and knowledge. Even though costs have risen, many feel that the improved quality of child care has been well worth it. The increased costs have been absorbed by increased charge to the customers and additional appropriated funds.

A Southern Paper Company.
The consulting firm WMS and Company, Inc. has a client (who wishes to remain nameless) who uses a broadbanded, skill-based incentive program along with its merit pay system to encourage employees to acquire skills and knowledge. (Although this is an example of both performance-based and skill-based pay, it is included in this section because of the interesting attributes of its skill-based pay system.) Job descriptions have been rewritten to include six to eight specific key end results with one to four different measures of accomplishment for each end result. Performance appraisals and performance-based base pay increases are based on these results. At the same time, a skill-based pay option is available to all employees. Employees who complete a training program and pass a rigorous test can either advance to a higher-level job, or, if there is no opening at the time, be placed in a higher "interim" pay range until an opening occurs. In either case, base pay is increased due to skills and knowledge acquired. The company has found this program successful because: (a) it has developed qualified workers in an unskilled labor market; (b) company-specific skills are taught to more employees, creating greater bench strength; and (c) morale and employee enthusiasm for the program are high (Meng, 1992). (It is not known whether general increases are given in this company.)

Northern Telecom.
Northern Telecom began its broadbanding system almost 5 years ago. Its program is one example of a skill-based system for white-collar work. The system's objectives are to improve customer satisfaction, increase employee commitment to Northern Telecom, and to place the entire company into one pay system.

Pay increases can be given for good performance, up to a target level. To go beyond the target level, employees must increase their skills. Northern Telecom uses "career development pay" to encourage employee development and to increase pay beyond the target level. This program has clearly defined skill sets. Higher-level skill sets include problem-solving abilities and interpersonal relations. Employees must demonstrate skill competency and are assessed by supervisors and peers before advancement. A matrix establishes a range for the amount of salary increase, but the specific amount of increase depends on the salary of peers, market data, and the level of risk the employee shows in the lateral move. A high-risk move, where very different skills and knowledge are needed (e.g., field technician to support engineer), deserves a higher increase in pay (LeBlanc, 1991).

No general increases are given to all employees, and so far there have been no range adjustments. If there were to be a range adjustment, a Northern Telecom spokesperson states that only the minimum and the maximum rates would change; individual employees would not receive the adjustment.

General Mills. Other than the manager, General Mills' Squeeze-It food-processing plants use only one job classification: operator/mechanic. Self-managed teams perform the continuous-process work. The work is broken into four skill blocks, with three levels in each block. Skill levels are defined in terms of performance required, area knowledge, and technical knowledge. Level 1 of each skill block indicates limited ability. Level 2 indicates partial proficiency, and Level 3 signifies that the employee is fully competent. Employees are expected to reach at least Level 2 in all four skill blocks. New employees begin at the entry rate and receive pay increases as they learn skill levels. Each skill level is worth a specified percentage pay increase. Peers appraise each other and determine skill competency. General Mills' strategy for adopting skill-based pay is: (a) to attract and retain a talented workforce; (b) to develop a salary structure competitive in the beverage industry; and (c) to ensure that the pay system reinforces organizational values and supports the work system and technology (Ledford et al., 1991). (It is not known whether general increases are given.)

Honeywell Ammunition Assembly Plant. For the past 9 years, the Honeywell Ammunition Assembly Plant has used skill-based pay for its production workforce. The system has gone through several revisions as a result of employee input. There are four defined skill blocks, with employees required to learn at least three. Employees are given 12 months to complete a skill block. Origin-ally, employees did not want to evaluate each other, but the program has evolved and peer input is now common (Ledford et al., 1991).

ESCA Corporation. ESCA Corporation, a small engineering firm located in Bellevue, Washington, has moved to a broadbanding system but refers to the bands as career paths. One reason for this change is that they use self-directed teams to accomplish the work. As part of this shift, the company determines salary or career advancement based on expanded knowledge, experience, and demonstrated career competencies. Workers can advance monetarily by demonstrating observable behaviors that are described in a set of career competency listings. Employees are evaluated by peers and leaders who observe and acknowledge their progress and achievement. Employee efforts will be recognized over time through the annual salary increase process. (Performance reviews are not the primary determinant for salary increase amounts, but they are considered.) A pay increase may be as high as 20 percent at the discretion of the team leader (Brown, 1993). (It is not known whether the company grants general increases to match range adjustments.)

Discussion

The categories of within-band pay progression strategies described here can be used individually or combined in a variety of ways. For instance, the broadbanding model recommended by the National Academy of Public Administration (NAPA) combines time-based and performance-based pay progression, with pay ranges divided into increments, similar to steps. Pay raises would be given once a year, with flexibility in the number of increments an employee could be given, based on performance and other relevant considerations (NAPA, 1991). This type of system is called a variable timing step-rate program and is often used as a transitional device to get from time-based pay to performance-based pay (Greene, 1991).

One author recommends using performance-based pay, but puts a different twist on it. Brookes suggests a performance contract system where an employer can promise to pay an increased amount of salary to an employee in exchange for a promise made by the employee to perform satisfactory future work of a specific and mutually agreed upon complexity. In this way, future performance becomes the focus, not past performance (Brookes, 1993).

The Monsanto Corporation uses a broadbanding system for its top management that is performance-based, but it also has a Nutra-Sweet division that has eliminated grades and bands altogether. Because pay is set and adjusted based on the market value of the job, NutraSweet relies heavily on gainsharing or incentive plans to reward employees. No across-the-board pay adjust-ments are given to all employees, but market adjustments may be made for particular occupations. Instead of receiving regular base pay increases, employees receive cash bonuses determined under specific incentive plans. Monsanto has over 40 different incentive plans that cover 25 percent of Monsanto's non-management workforce.

Summary

Because of the wide variation in agency missions, work assignments, cultures, and environments, one broadbanding system with one pay progression strategy will not meet the needs of the entire Federal government. It may be most effective to enable agencies to select an approach from among a range of broadbanding and pay progression strategies that fits their specific situation and promotes improved organizational performance.

Through the Hewitt survey, companies using broadbanding systems gave advice to others thinking of adopting the system. Based on their experiences, these companies advised: (a) put strong emphasis on communication and education; (b) make clear distinctions about how pay increases are determined; (c) be sure to integrate the program with the career development function (not solely compensation); and (d) be extra sensitive to any groups of employees who may get hurt when moving to bands (Gerson, 1992). The

Hay Group also advises caution and thorough analysis. If banding is simply tacked on to rigid systems of pay and employer/employee relationships, it will probably fail (Hay Group, 1992).

There can be many advantages to establishing a well-planned broadbanding system in an organization with the appropriate climate, culture, and environment. Broadbanding can break down many of the nagging but often hidden barriers to teamwork and cooperation. Continuous improvement and teams do not operate effectively in a culture that places too much emphasis on hierarchy (LeBlanc, 1992).

Finally, it is worth noting in a discussion on pay strategies that base pay should be consider-ed only part of an organization's compensation strategy. Variable pay, group incentives, gain-sharing, etc., can all be used effectively to manage employee performance and should be integrated into the total direct compensation picture (McNally, 1992).

References

Abosch, Kenan S. and Janice S. Hand, *Broadbanding Design, Approaches and Practices*, American Compensation Association, Scottsdale, AZ, 1994.

American Compensation Association and American Society for Personnel Administration (ACA/ASPA), *Elements of Sound Base Pay Administration*, 2nd Edition, American Compensation Associa-tion, Scottsdale, AZ, 1988.

Braddick, Carol A., Michael B. Jones, and Paul M. Shafer, "A Look at Broadband-ing in Practice," *Journal of Compensation and Benefits*, July-August 1992.

Brown, David L., "Self-Directed Work Teams: Employee Empowerment at ESCA Corp.," *ACA Journal*, Spring/Summer 1993.

Brookes, Donald, "Merit Pay: Does It Help or Hinder Productivity?," *HRFocus*, January 1993.

Deming, W. Edwards, *Quality, Productivity and Competitive Position*, Massachusetts Institute of Technology, Cambridge, MA, 1982.

Eyes, Peter R., "Realignment Ties Pay to Performance," *Personnel Journal*, Janu-ary 1993.

Froiland, Paul, "Reproducing Star Performers," *Training*, September 1993.

Gerson, Sareen R., "Broadbanding Study Re-veals New Interest in Private Sector," *Clas-sifiers' Column*, May-June 1992.

Gerson, Sareen R., "NAPA Study Revisited," *Classifiers' Column*, May-June 1992.

Graber, Jim M., Roger E. Breisch, and Wal-ter E. Breisch, "Performance Appraisals and Deming: A Misunder-standing?," *Quality Progress*, June 1992.

Greene, Robert J., and Ann D. Scott, "Alter-natives to Time-Based Pay," *Public Per-sonnel Management*, Vol. 20 No. 4, Winter 1991.

The Hay Group, "The Hay Report: Compen-sation and Benefits Strategies for 1993 and Beyond," The Hay Group, Philadel-phia, PA, 1992.

Hofrichter, David, "Broadbanding: A 'Sec-ond Generation' Approach," *Compensa-tion and Benefits Review*, September-Oc-tober 1993.

Jenkins, G. Douglas, Jr., Gerald E. Ledford, Jr., Nina Gupta, and D. Harold Doty, *Skill-Based Pay: Practices, Payoffs, Pitfalls and Prescriptions*, American Compensation Association, Scottsdale, AZ, 1992.

Lawler, Edward E., III, "Pay the Person, Not the Job," *Industry Week*, December 7, 1992.

Lawler, Edward E., III, Gerald E. Ledford, Jr., and Lei Chang, "Who Uses Skill-Based Pay, and Why," *Compensation and Benefits Review*, March-April 1993.

LeBlanc, Peter V., "Pay-Banding Can Help Align Pay with New Organizational Structures," *National Productivity Review*, Summer 1992.

LeBlanc, Peter V., "Skill-Based Pay Case Number 2: Northern Telecom," *Compensation and Benefits Review*, March-April 1991.

Ledford, Gerald E., Jr., "Three Case Studies on Skill-Based Pay: An Overview," *Compensation and Benefits Review,* March-April 1991.

Ledford, Gerald E., Jr., and Gary Bergel, "Skill-Based Pay Case Number 1: General Mills," *Compensation and Benefits Review,* March-April 1991.

Ledford, Gerald E., Jr., William R. Tyler and William B. Dixey, "Skill-Based Pay Case Number 3: Honeywell Ammunition Assembly Plant," *Compensation and Benefits Review,* March-April 1991.

McCarthy, Eugene Michael, "The 'Banding' Concept," *Classifiers' Column*, May/June 1993.

McNally, Kathleen A., "Compensation as a Strategic Tool," *HRMagazine*, July 1992.

Meng, G. Jonathan, "Using Job Descriptions, Performance and Pay Innovations to Support Quality: A Paper Company's Experience," *National Productivity Review*, Spring 1992.

National Academy of Public Administration (NAPA), *Modernizing Federal Classification: An Opportunity for Excellence*, NAPA, Washington, DC, July 1991.

The National Performance Review, *From Red Tape to Results: Creating a Government That Works Better & Costs Less*, Washington, DC, September 1993.

National Research Council (NRC), *Pay for Performance: Evaluating Performance*

Appraisal and Merit Pay, National Academy Press, Washington, DC, 1991.

Pay-For-Performance Labor-Management Committee (PFPLMC), *Strengthening the Link Between Pay and Performance*, U.S. Office of Personnel Management, Washington, DC, November 1991.

Reynolds, Douglas, Margaret Barton, Mary Beth Terry, George Thornton, Kevin Murphy, and Anthony Bayless, *Fourth Annual Evaluation Report: National Institute of Standards and Technology Personnel Management Demonstration Project*, U.S. Office of Personnel Management, Washington, DC, December 1992.

Rivenbark, Leigh, "Pay Banding Experiments Prove Successful," *Federal Times*, April 19, 1993.

Schay, Brigitte W., *Broad-Banding in the Federal Government: Management Report*, U.S. Office of Personnel Management, Washington, DC, February 1993.

Schay, Brigitte W., "Broad-Banding in the Federal Government," *The Public Manager*, Summer 1993.

Schneier, Craig Eric and Richard W. Beatty, "What Is Performance Appraisal?", *The Performance Appraisal Sourcebook*, Baird, Beatty and Schneier (Eds), Human Resource Development Press, Amherst, MA, 1982.

Scholtes, Peter R., "An Elaboration of Deming's Teaching on Performance Appraisal," Joiner Associates, Inc., Madison, Wisconsin, 1987.

U.S. Office of Personnel Management (OPM), "Pacer Share: A Federal Productivity and Personnel Management Demonstration Project (Fourth-Year Evaluation Report)," U.S. Office of Personnel Management, Washington, DC, December 1992.

U.S. Office of Personnel Management (OPM), "Performance Management and Recognition System: 1992-1993 Annual Report," U.S. Office of Personnel Management, Washington, DC, September 1995.

U.S. Office of Personnel Management (OPM), "Status of the Evaluation of the Navy Personnel Management Demonstration Project: Management Report I," U.S. Office of Personnel Management, Washington, DC, March 1984.

U.S. Office of Personnel Management (OPM), *Survey of Federal Employees*, U.S. Office of Personnel Management, Washington, DC, May 1992.

Verespej, Michael A., "Pay-For-Skills: Its Time Has Come," *Industry Week*, June 15, 1992.

Appendix

Major Contributors to this Report

Doris Hausser, Chief
Performance Management and
**   Incentive Awards Division**

Karen Lebing
Personnel Management Specialist
Performance Management and
**   Incentive Awards Division**

www.ingramcontent.com/pod-product-compliance
Lightning Source LLC
Chambersburg PA
CBHW081413170526
45166CB00010B/3320